Anger Management For Kids 5-8 Years Old

A Brief Guide To Understand The Reasons And Causes Behind Your Kids Aggression With Effective Tips And Techniques To Help Kids Overcome It

Theodora Hewitt

book are for clarifying purposes only and are owned by the owners themselves, not affiliated with this document.

Contents

Introduction

Anger is a natural and spontaneous reaction to danger. Our survival necessitates a certain amount of rage. When you have difficulties managing your anger, it might lead to you saying or doing things you later regret. Anger that is out of control is harmful to one's physical and mental health. It can also swiftly escalate into verbal or physical violence, causing harm to yourself and others. Anger can be triggered by a variety of factors, including stress, family troubles, and financial concerns. Anger can be triggered by an underlying condition such as depression in kids. Anger isn't considered a problem in and of itself, but it is a symptom of a number of mental illnesses. Anger can be a sign of depression, which is defined as a period of melancholy and loss of interest that lasts at least two weeks. Anger can be restrained or expressed openly. The amount of anger and the manner in which it is displayed differs from one person to the next. Other signs of depression include irritation, a lack of energy, thoughts of hopelessness, and so on. Obsessive-Compulsive Disorder (OCD) is associated with a lot of anger (OCD). It affects almost half of all OCD sufferers. Anger might arise as a consequence of irritation with your inability to stop obsessive thoughts as well as compulsive activities or as a consequence of someone or something interfering with your capacity to perform a ritual. Disorders such as Attention Deficit Hyperactivity Disorder (ADHD) are also caused by anger (ADHD). Inattention, hyperactivity, and/or impulsivity are signs of this neurodevelopmental condition. Symptoms normally begin in early childhood and last for the rest of one's life. Some people are not diagnosed with ADHD until they are adults. This is referred to as adult ADHD. Anger and irritability are common in people with ADHD of all ages. Other signs and symptoms include restlessness, difficulty concentrating, and poor time management and planning abilities. Oppositional defiant disorder (ODD) is a behavioral condition that affects 1 to 16% of children in school. Anger, impatience, and a hot temper are all common indicators of ODD. Others can easily irritate children with ODD. They may be obstinate and aggressive. Bipolar disorder can be caused by a child's anger. It's a neurological condition that produces mood swings that are extreme. Although not everyone with bipolar disorder will suffer depression, these severe mood fluctuations can range from mania to depression. Anger, impatience, and wrath are common among children with bipolar illness. During a depressive episode, children may experience sadness, hopelessness, tears, and a loss of interest in previously appreciated activities. Anger can also cause a child to develop IED (Intermittent Explosive Disorder). IED (Intermittent explosive disorder) is a condition in which a kid exhibits aggressive, impulsive, or violent conduct on a regular basis. He or she could overreact to situations by erupting in rage that is out of proportion to the circumstances. Temper tantrums, disagreements, fighting, physical violence, and throwing things are all frequent behaviors. In children, one of the stages of sorrow is anger. The death of a loved one, a divorce, or a breakup can all cause grief. The individual who died, anyone else involved in the event, or inanimate things may all be targets of rage. Shock, sadness, loneliness, and fear are some of the other signs of grieving. There are a lot of emotions that are linked to rage. Irritability, impatience, worry, rage, and tension are some of the emotional signs you may sense before, during, or after an angry outburst. Consider seeking treatment from a mental health professional if you fear your child's anger is out of control or is negatively affecting your life or relationships. Learning how to handle an aggressive child with behavioral approaches might be difficult for parents, but it may make a great impact on many children. Parents who are calm, confident, and consistent can help their children learn the skills they need to control their own behavior. This may take more patience and willingness to try new tactics than with a typically developing child, but the payoff is well worth the effort when the result is a better relationship and a happier home.

Chapter 1: Reasons and Symptoms for Anger in Kids 5-8 Years Old

Irritability in children is defined as a higher proclivity to rage as compared to their peers. It shows up in the form of developmentally unsuitable anger outbursts and a morose, grumpy mood in clinical settings. As a result, it encompasses both mood and behavioral elements. Mood dysregulation, which comprises just behavioral manifestations, and aggression, which is bigger than irritation, are related categories. Disruptive Mood Dysregulation Disorder (DMDD) is a childhood disorder characterized by severe irritation, wrath, and frequent, violent outbursts of temper. DMDD symptoms are more than just being a cranky kid; children with DMDD have a serious impairment that necessitates medical intervention. Anger proneness follows a predictable developmental path, peaking in preschool and then falling, with a small uptick during adolescence. Irritability is a popular cause for children's mental health evaluations, and irritability in children is linked to both present and future impairment.

1.1 Studies On Pediatric Bipolar Disorder

Pediatric bipolar disorder, according to American researchers in the 1990s, does not show with identifiable manic episodes like adult bipolar illness, but rather with severe, persistent irritability.

Posthoc analysis of epidemiological research, on the other hand, identified links between childhood irritability and the likelihood of anxiety and depression later in life, but not bipolar disorder. Similarly, studies examining the two components of oppositional defiant disorder (ODD), headstrong and irritability behavior, have found that irritability predicts eventual depression and anxiety, but headstrong behavior predicts ADHD and conduct disorder. As a result, rather than persistent irritability, the bipolar disorder must be diagnosed in children and adults who have distinct manic episodes. Irritability and depression have been linked in genetic studies. Longitudinal relationships between irritability and depression and anxiety have a hereditary component, according to twin studies. These studies also discovered that irritability has a heritability of 40-60%, equivalent to unipolar depression or anxiety. Irritability is a diagnostic standard for a variety of diseases in children and adolescents, including anxiety conditions, major depressive disorder, as well as oppositional defiant disorder (ODD). It's also frequent in children and teenagers with ADHD, conduct disorder, bipolar disorder, or autism. The clinical relevance and validity of a diagnostic category marked predominantly by irritability in children and adolescents, on the other hand, remains a significant and unsolved concern. That category has traditionally been ODD, which is defined as a disruptive behavior disorder. ODD, on the other hand, is made up of 2 dimensions, one of which, irritability, has genetically mediated longitudinal links to depression and anxiety. Severe irritability has also been linked to anxiety disorders in a cross-sectional study. These arguments put into question whether merging irritable and headstrong characteristics into one disease is appropriate and whether a diagnosis marked primarily by irritability should be classified as an externalizing and disruptive behavior disorder rather than a mood illness. The pathophysiology of irritation can be studied using two neuroscience-based formulations. Irritability is defined as an abnormal reaction to irritation; the emotion evoked when a goal is hindered, such as when an anticipated reward is delayed. The second view of irritability is that it is an abnormal approach to threat: although healthy creatures approach a threat (that is, attack) only when it is unavoidable, irritable people may attack in a wider range of situations. Threat and frustration combine in defining an animal's behavior in an animal model with translational promise for researching irritability. Specifically, those that experienced frustrative non-reward (that is, it did not get an expected prize) displayed higher motor activity and were more likely to outbreak a conspecific than no frustrated rodents. This hyperactivity and heightened proclivity for aggressiveness could be compared to the behavior of a frustrated toddler having a temper tantrum. Irritability and brain reactions to frustration (for example, rigged games) and threat have been studied using functional magnetic resonance imaging (e.g., annoyed faces). Interactions between dysfunction and irritability in the amygdala, anterior cingulate cortex, striatum, and parietal lobe have been found, which is consistent with irritable teens' deficiencies in reward processing and maintaining control when frustrated. Irritable children are also more prone than their non-irritable peers to interpret vague faces as angry and, like children with anxiety disorders, to pay attention to angry faces first. Identifying the extent to which impairments in return or threat processing distinguish subtypes of irritable adolescents is one direction for future research.

Also, whether the brain mechanisms that mediate irritability differ between findings and/or when irritability coexists with another feature, such as anxiety, is a key concern. Early evidence suggests that the pathophysiology of irritation differs depending on the situation. Because DMDD was just recently included in DSM5, there are just a few controlled trials. However, research concentrated on irritability in the setting of other diseases, such as ADHD as well as major depressive disorder, has led to some preliminary recommendations. Stimulants have been shown to lessen irritability in children with ADHD. While stimulants are generally contraindicated in bipolar disorder, they might well be beneficial in the treatment of DMDD. The use of atypical antipsychotic medication in children with irritability and autism, as well as in children with aggression, is supported by research. Recent rises in antipsychotic prescriptions, on the other hand, may have stemmed in part from efforts to manage pediatric irritability without proper consideration of alternate pharmacologic and psychotherapy treatments. In adults, selective serotonin reuptake inhibitors (SSRIs) may be used to treat irritability; the longitudinal correlations and high comorbidity between anxiety, irritability, and depression suggest such an approach in children. In the treatment of irritability, psychotherapeutic techniques are likely to be essential. Parental teaching can reduce a child's hostility as well as irritability. Implicit training to change irritable children's propensity to see ambiguous faces as angry is being investigated, as is cognitive-behavioral techniques. The increased focus on irritation has provided a wealth of information concerning its long-term trajectory and links to psychopathology. The goal of ongoing research is to understand the brain processes that mediate irritability and use that information to develop new therapeutic options.

1.2 What Actually Triggers Anger In Kids?

It's vital to remember that anger is a healthy and normal emotion when it's expressed properly. However, if your child or student has frequent angry outbursts or is growing aggressive, it may be time for you to become an anger detective. Understanding the source of the anger is the greatest place to start when trying to treat an angry kid. When it comes to the things that make children angry, it's vital to remember that kids aren't all that different from adults. It's simply that their responses are usually so raw. They haven't yet mastered all of the self-control and coping skills which we grownups have. As a result, everything comes to a head swiftly and in full force. To assist your child in coping with feelings of anger, you must first determine why the child is angry, as the optimal reaction for each circumstance may differ. Don't be fooled by your child's anger; it serves a protective function for them as well. The unconscious mind of your child directs your child's anger. Anger is neither good nor harmful; it is necessary for living. Angry children aren't all terrible. An angry child is doing the best they can to manage and survive at the time. There's always a reason for a child's anger issues, even if we're often so shaken by angry behaviors that we don't delve deep enough to locate it in our rapid reactions. The first step in assisting a child in dealing with anger in a healthy manner is to identify the underlying causes and treat the source of the problem. The first step in helping your angry child deal with their anger in a better way is to become curious about them and what problems may lie under their aggressive and intense behaviors. While pinpointing the exact cause of each and every eruption of anger is not always easy, there are numerous typical reasons why a child might struggle to control anger in daily life.

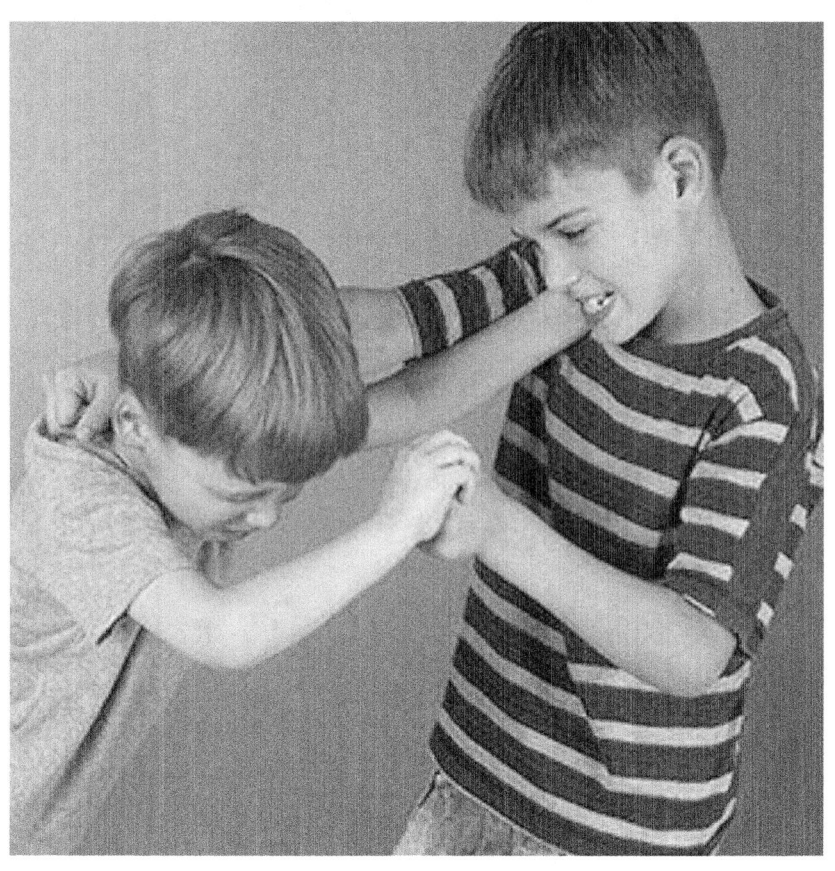

1.2.1 Look for triggers

Start to notice when they become angry and what causes their outbursts. You might even want to jot down some notes for yourself about what happened just before the child's angry outburst, what the kid did, how you replied, and what eventually helped the child calm down. It may also be beneficial to assess the child's anger on a scale of 1-10 to remember the severity or to ask the kid to assess their personal anger on a scale.

1.2.2 Find patterns

Read over the notes and seek trends after a few angry outbursts. It's crucial to remember that even if we don't believe the trigger is significant, it may be significant to the child. It's vital to recognize your children's feelings and embrace and allow their anger if you want them to be emotionally healthy in the long run. That doesn't imply you should accept undesirable means of expressing yourself, such as aggression or negative comments, but it does involve empathizing with the feelings rather than trying to suppress them.

1.2.3 Developmental Growth Spurt

When it comes to the child's development and growth, you've probably heard of physical "growing pains," but you've probably never heard of emotional "growing pains." Certain ages and phases of development are associated with rapid brain development, and as with any major renovation, considerable construction may be required. During the developmental strides of toddlerhood, late childhood, and adolescence, your child's neurons and synapses will be hard at work, but they will be unable to use parts of the brain that manage self-control as well as emotional regulation.

1.2.4 There is an underlying medical condition

This is a significant yet frequently overlooked cause of kid violence and anger. If your child appears angry as well as aggressive more frequently than you believe "normal," you must consult with the pediatrician. And don't be surprised if the answer isn't simple or quick to find. You may start helping your child heal once you figure out why he or she is angry.

1.2.5 They're physically uncomfortable

This is one of the simple patterns to spot. Were they wiping their eyes, yawning, or hyperactive and demonstrating less physical control than normal before the outburst? Most likely, they're simply exhausted. You can give the child a nap. Suggestions for quiet rest time include lying down and listening to music. Read some stories while snuggled up.

1.2.6 Your child is extremely tired

This is particularly evident when children are babies and toddlers, who require naps and 13-hour sleep cycles at night. However, do not dismiss the 7-year-old who has stayed up late a couple of nights and gone to school every day for a week. She has the potential to be pretty frightening. Children's brains and bodies are still developing to the point where they can't afford to go without sleep for long periods of time. And while we appear to respect this theory when our children are infants, did you know that even your five-year-old requires between 10 and 11 hours of sleep per night? Don't presume your child is actually angry until you've confirmed she's gotten enough sleep.

1.2.7 Signs they're angry because they're hungry

If you notice your child is frequently hungry or angry after going without meals for an extended period of time, you may have a kid who is sensitive to low blood sugar. You can fetch them a fast snack like half a glass of juice or a little piece of cheese to help with the low-blood sugar symptoms. In the long run, consider serving meals earlier in the day or healthy snack options with both protein and carbohydrates, which will provide a longer as well as the slower release of energy as compared to high carbohydrate or sugary foods, which metabolize faster and can cause a drop in blood sugar.

1.2.8 Big life events like trauma

Change as well as loss is inevitable in life, as is the anger that can accompany them. For a kid, seemingly normal changes such as starting pre-school can cause an upheaval in their daily routine, which can be disconcerting and lead to increased emotionality. When a child's emotion center is strongly stimulated, he or she will be less able to access their "thinking brain," which may normally serve to interrupt angry impulses.

1.2.9 Behavioral challenges

Many children are born with emotional and behavioral issues that have a significant impact on their ability to comprehend and manage anger. These problems are almost usually visible from a young age and are very persistent throughout life. ADHD, Sensory Processing Issues, and Autism are just a few examples of developmental problems that can make it difficult for a child to manage his or her emotions.

1.2.10 Temperament and personality

We know that around half of a child's personality is hard-wired from birth, and any parent of a strong-willed child understands that certain children are naturally less adaptable than their peers. Because they experience emotions more frequently as well as intensely in everyday life, many sensitive, energetic, intense, and highly emotional kids have to work harder to regulate their major emotions.

1.2.11 Physical causes

Low blood sugar, lack of proper sleep, as well as other physical health issues can all play a part in your child's ability to manage his or her anger. A child's mental health is intimately linked to their physical health, which means that little daily changes like getting enough sleep as well as spending more time in nature can either exacerbate or enhance a child's mood and behavior.

1.2.12 Learning challenges and disabilities

When a child has an undetected learning problem, frustration and anger are common reactions. When a child's ability does not match the expectations placed on them by others, it can lead to a persistent cycle of anger, stress, and frustration, especially if the cause is unknown.

1.2.13 They get angry because they are overstimulated

Did they have an outburst after being agitated, angry, or spacing out and/or exhausted after being in a loud or bustling environment? Allow them to de-stimulate by providing them with space, calm, dark, or an activity in which they can vent their fury. Play dough, sketching paper, cushions to throw, TV, soft music, story time, or a warm bath are all good options. Offer a variety of options and discover what your child prefers. This is a common source of anger in youngsters who are hypersensitive or on the autism spectrum. Environments that you don't mind may temporarily overburden their system.

1.2.14 They feel powerless and out of control

"Sit here and be quiet." "Get dressed and clean your teeth." "For dinner, we have spaghetti." When you think about it, we give our children a lot of instructions but not a lot of options. Part of this is due to the fact that we are the parents, and we simply cannot allow our children to dictate all of our choices since nothing (productive) would be done. But, when you think about it, telling our children what to do is just easier. After a while, our children may feel as if they have no voice, which can be disheartening. We attempt to provide as many opportunities for our girls to make their own decisions as possible. It's all about the little things - Every morning; they dress. They contribute to our weekly meal plan, so their favorites are prepared frequently. It's nothing significant, but it gives them a feeling of power. It can also swiftly assist you in determining the true cause of your child's anger because they will have greater faith in you. Anger is a simple way for the subconscious mind to capture a sense of power for many of us. Children in today's environment spend a significant portion of their day obeying the orders of others. Due to busy schedules as well as long hours at school and extracurricular activities, children have less time for child-directed play, which has long been used to help children develop a healthy sense of control and power. Anger is a simple way for children to communicate their feelings of powerlessness. "No!" you hear. "That is something I do not want." That is something I do not wish to do. Power conflicts, digging in one's heels, the kid refusing to cooperate, and so on are all visible. You're enraged or threatened by their actions. Nobody, including children, enjoys being in charge. Give your kid as much power as possible in a healthy way. Allow them to make more decisions, give them responsibilities in life, teach more skills so that they can become as self-sufficient as possible, ask for their opinion more frequently, refuse to cooperate in power struggles, describe your expectations, allow natural consequences for their choices, or ask for assistance. On a daily basis, kid's power quotas must be met.

1.2.15 They feel disconnected

Were they overly attached before they became angry? Were they pushing you for things or requesting that you play with them? Were you irritated by what they were doing? Most likely, they're angry because they don't feel connected to you. Spend additional time interacting with the child over the next few days and weeks. Empathize with what they're going through. Remember that in order to feel comfortable and loved, kids require at least 10 to 20 minutes of pure, connect time each day where they receive their entire attention without the use of technology or other distractions. The biological urge for a child to have a deep, warm, as well as connected relationship with a caregiver is strong. It gives your child a sense of safety, allowing him or her to explore and learn in order to attain healthy development. If a child's need for connection isn't filled, anger is a common way for him or her to express that desire to adults. When a kid doesn't feel seen or heard, they will utilize behavior and speech to try harder to be seen and heard.

1.2.16 They feel misunderstood

You hear your child remark, "You never listen to me, that's not what I said," and you think to yourself, "Why don't you ever listen to me, or stop interrupting me?" Or perhaps your child was attempting to communicate with you, you answered, and then they became silent and angry. Learn how to listen in different ways so that your children feel heard. These abilities may not come naturally to us, but they may make a huge impact on our kid's development.

1.2.17 They feel hurt

Instead of conveying that their feelings have been hurt, some kids lash out aggressively to retaliate and exact retribution. You can hear something like, "I despise you" or "I don't love you." If you believe their feelings have been hurt, try identifying and empathizing with the underlying root of their anger by saying, "You seem incredibly agitated or are your feelings hurt?" "Did I or somebody else do or say something that hurt your feelings?" you might ask. You may become extremely angry as a result of this. When the child has cooled down, have a chat with him or her and underline that it's fine to be angry, but it's not appropriate to call him or her names or act aggressively to express it. Teach them how to express themselves using "I" statements.

1.2.18 They are displacing the anger

This type of anger may emerge at the conclusion of a long day at school or during a visit with family or friends. Outbursts may arise "out of nowhere" in reaction to something seemingly insignificant. Displaced anger is frequently the result of a build-up of minor tensions and upsets that have been suppressed – till one final tiny stressor pushes the kid over the edge. Imagine a glass gently filling with drips of water throughout the day that doesn't overflow until the very last drop. Displaced anger usually emerges when children finally feel comfortable expressing their disappointed feelings. If this happens every day towards the conclusion of the school day, talk to your child's teacher about it so you can come up with strategies to help the day run more smoothly. Alternatively, the smartest thing you can do is accept that you are not the source of the child's anger and that the kid is simply venting his or her frustrations. Labeling the anger, empathizing, listening, and assisting them in finding a healthy outlet for the stress are the finest things you can do.

1.2.19 Kids' boundaries have been invaded

If children feel physically controlled or invaded, such as when their wrists are grasped, picked up, or otherwise physically handled, or if they are hugged or kissed when they don't want it, they may become angry. They may become angry if their emotional boundaries have been breached (someone has put them down, made a critical remark to them, or excluded them). It's critical to understand that this is a rational response. When one's boundaries have been crossed, an uncomfortable emotional response is an instinctively protective reflex. It's also a better answer than a child who doesn't defend his or her boundaries at all. Teach children to use the I statement to clearly convey their boundaries to others.

1.2.20 They start displaying anxiety

The majority of parents are unaware that anxiety symptoms in children resemble anger issues. A child experiencing anxiety will become angrier more rapidly and frequently because their brain feels under siege and also has gone into 'fight or flight' mode. Kids that are angry are frequently showing that feeling as a result of underlying anxiety. Anger is simpler to regulate since it releases adrenaline into the body, which can feel powerful and empowering rather than out of control. Try to chat to them about how they felt before they became furious after the outburst has passed. Empathize with the child and pay attention to him. Make a list of activities they can do to make themselves feel better when they're anxious.

1.2.21 Failing to get what the kids want to make them frustrated!

The classic temper tantrum is a term used to describe this type of anger. Essentially, the child is having trouble dealing with his or her disappointment. Alternately, throwing a temper tantrum has helped them achieve what they want, so they're doing it again. This one is usually simple to figure out in either case. You've identified your reason if the anger is aroused when they ask for something and are subsequently denied, especially if you give in and modify your decision after their outburst. If your decision to refuse your child something has resulted in an angry outburst, the best thing you can do is stick to your guns and ride out the storm. If you change your mind after the child has been angry, you are rewarding the behavior and encouraging them to try to manipulate you again the next time you say no. You can empathize with, and allow, your child's anger and frustration without giving in, whether or not it was your decision that upset them. Just because your children are upset doesn't mean we have to try to distract them or make them feel better. Empathizing with them allows them to ride out the emotion, and as they grow older, they will build their own coping strategies to help them deal with frustration more effectively.

1.2.22 Anger is modeled

The behaviors which parents manifest for their children is a great teacher and the most effective technique to help an angry kid. It's simple to understand how a child may pick up similar coping mechanisms if anger is frequently permitted to influence adult behavior in the home. What a child sees and observes on a daily basis is a powerful teacher, whether anger is used as a tactic to get a child's cooperation or adults in the family do not effectively manage as well as model healthy anger coping skills.

1.3 More Reasons Behind Your Child's Anger

Some misbehavior in children may be the result of negative attention-seeking or full-fledged anger outbursts. These aren't the consequence of a personality conflict, nor are they the product of boredom. It's important to keep in mind that anger is an emotion of secondary nature. Anger is employed as a secondary emotion for a variety of reasons.

- In American society, anger is a normal emotion. Aggression and violence can be found in a variety of media, including television, music, toys, and, of course, video games.

- Because of the endorphins released by our nervous system and the physical/mental distance it creates between us and others, anger can be employed as a means to protect us from emotional suffering.

According to behavior modification therapy, we can change behavior by changing the antecedent (what happens before the behavior) or the consequence (what happens after the behavior) (what transpires immediately after the behavior). We must address the antecedent or source of anger because it is a product of primary emotions. The following is a list of possible places to investigate in order to figure out what is causing the children's anger.

1.3.1 Sadness

Sadness could be because of:

- Parents frequent heated debates

- Best friend moving

- Death

- Change in schools

- Parent deployment

- No one to play with

- Divorce

- A parent working long hours

1.3.2 Fear

Fear could be because of:

- Worry about enough food

- Worry about a house and ancillary requirements
- Sick parents
- Sick family member
- Personal illness
- Fear of becoming the victim of physical or emotional or sexual abuse
- Fear of a family member becoming the victim of physical or emotional or sexual abuse
- Loved one doing a dangerous job (police, military, firefighter)
- Worry about the shortage of funds for payment of bills

1.3.3 Frustration

Frustration might stem from:
- Poor academic performance
- Poor social skills
- Lack of physical abilities
- Speech problems
- Comparison with high-performing siblings
- The feeling of lack of control

1.3.4 Guilt

A guild could be a result of:
- Sexual abuse victimization
- Letting someone down
- Guilt for a divorce

- Sense of responsibility for a death
- Hurt a loved one (emotionally or physically)
- Failure to comply with directions

1.3.5 Disappointment

Disappointment could be because of the following reasons:
- Was not invited to a party
- Was not chosen for a group activity
- Was not selected in the team
- Could not win the game
- Poor grades
- Parent not keeping up promises
- Change in family plans
- Financial limitations

1.3.6 Worry

The following could be the reasons for a kid's anxious behavior:
- Basic needs of food, shelter and health
- Family personal use of alcohol
- Family mental health
- Violence
- Bullying
- Uncertainty

1.3.7 Embarrassment

The child may feel embarrassed because of:

- Socializing and performing in front of peer group
- Physical looks
- Feeling lowly and stupid
- Feeling worthless

1.3.8 Jealousy

The reasons for jealousy could be:

- Friends of friends
- Siblings
- Class fellows
- Parents' time and exclusive attention
- Social status

1.3.9 Hurt

Feelings of hurt could trigger from the following factors:

- Abandonment
- Rejection
- Peer betrayal
- Preferred sibling
- Break-up of a friendship
- Family betrayal
- Boyfriend or girlfriend break-up

1.3.10 Anxiety

The kid may display anxiety because of:

- Inconsistency
- Social pressure
- Personal expectations
- Poor boundaries
- School performance
- Anxiety disorders

1.3.11 Shame

Shame is generally a result of the following factors:

- Low academic performance
- Inability to match the expectations of others
- Emotional, sexual and physical abuse
- Frequent disciplinary actions
- Finding it challenging to control behavior

1.4 Symptoms That Your Kid Is Suffering From Anger

Some children appear to have a short fuse from birth. When they are unhappy, they may become impatient, intolerant, or confrontational. It can be unpleasant for the entire family to deal with erratic behavior. While it's natural for toddlers to have temper tantrums as well as preschoolers to lash out at times, it's crucial to keep an eye out for behavior that isn't typical of children of their age. These warning flags may signal that your child requires professional assistance.

1.4.1 Difficulty with relationships

It's natural for young children to hit a sibling or call someone a name now and again. When children's angry outbursts, on the other hand, prevent them from establishing friendships or from developing good connections with family members, it's time to take action.

1.4.2 Disruption of family life

In your own home, you shouldn't have to tread carefully. It is not healthy for everyone in the family if your everyday activities are disrupted due to your child's angry behavior. Skipping trips or giving in to the child to avoid a tantrum are only short-term solutions that will result in long-term issues. If you're missing out on fun activities or having trouble spending one-on-one time with another child, your child's behavior has to be addressed.

1.4.3 Aggression

Aggression should be used only when all other options have been exhausted. However, for children with anger issues, usually lashing out at others is the first line of defense. When kids have difficulty solving problems, resolving conflicts, or asking for help, they may resort to aggression to meet their needs. Teaching new skills might sometimes help a child realize that violent behavior isn't always essential.

1.4.4 Immature behavior

While it's normal for 2-year-olds to fall on the ground and kick their feet when they're angry, this is not the case for an 8-year-old. As your child grows older, the frequency and intensity of his or her meltdowns should lessen. If your child's temper tantrums are becoming more frequent, it's an indication that they're having problems managing their emotions.

1.4.5 Frequent frustration

As children grow older, they should be able to handle more frustrating activities. If a 7-year-old throws their building toys when their creations topple over, or if a 9-year-old crushes their papers each time they make a mistake on their homework, it's a sign that they need help with frustration tolerance.

Chapter 2: Causes of Aggression in Kids 5-8 Years Old

Aggression in kids can be a sign of a variety of underlying issues. It's a really polymorphic phenomenon, a commonality for a wide range of psychiatric disorders, medical issues, and life situations. So the first step in treating aggression is to figure out what's causing it. Aggression is caused by a variety of factors that can be classified into numerous categories.

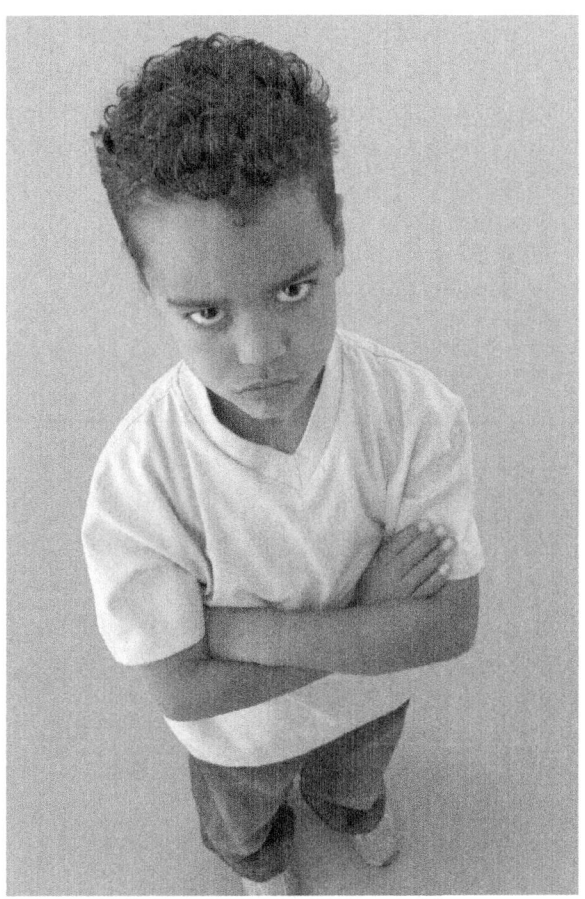

2.1 Mood Disorders

Mood disorders are at the root of kid's aggression. Bipolar kids who are in their manic episodes are frequently aggressive. They lose control of themselves and become impulsive. On the other hand, when they grow melancholy, they might become irritable, and this irritability and cantankerousness can prompt kids to lash out, albeit aggression is less common.

2.2 Psychosis

Aggression can be a symptom of psychotic illnesses. Children with schizophrenia, for example, frequently respond to internal sensations that might be distressing. Sometimes children with schizophrenia become suspicious or paranoid, and they strike out because of their own fear.

2.3 Frustration

Aggression is a symptom of cognitive impairment, also known as intellectual impairment or communication (including autism) in children. When children with these illnesses become aggressive, it's usually because they're having trouble coping with their anxiety as well as irritation and can't express themselves like others. Aggression could also be a manifestation of impulsivity.

2.4 Impulsivity

Then there are the issues with a disruptive behavior disorder. Impulsivity as well as poor decision-making in children with ADHD, the most frequent of the disorders, can lead to aggressive behavior. These kids frequently do not consider the repercussions of their behavior, which can make them appear callous or nasty when they are simply not thinking.

2.5 Conduct Disorder

Aggression is a large part of what conduct disorder is, and it is part of the matrix of the illness. Children with CD, unlike children who simply do not consider the consequences of their actions, are deliberately malicious, and their treatment, as well as prognosis, are very different.

2.6 Injury

When a child suffers from frontal lobe damage or certain types of epilepsy, there are sometimes organic reasons for aggressive outbursts. There may be no clear and understandable reason for the aggressive episode in these cases, and the episode could be explosive.

2.7 Trauma

Finally, aggression in kids and teenagers can be triggered by stressors in their environment rather than an underlying emotional illness. However, it's important to remember that this is a rare occurrence, and when aggression becomes more frequent, it could indicate a developing emotional problem.

2.8 Warning Signs That Your Child Is Under Stress

Children become more stressed as they grow older as well as take on new tasks, participate in more activities, and have more homework loads. Take a look at these warning signs that the child might be dealing with stress.

2.8.1 Nightmares

Fear that arises during sleep is a common reaction to tense or traumatic events. Telling your kid stories about other children who have experienced similar emotions can make them feel better. It shows them that you are aware of their feelings.

2.8.2 Trouble focusing and completing schoolwork

Social and academic pressures, particularly the desire to fit in, are major stressors for children. While extracurricular activities could be a good way to relieve stress, over-scheduling can make things worse. Assist your child in properly balancing his priorities.

2.8.3 Increased aggression

When children are stressed, they may react physically (kicking, biting, or hitting) or manifest verbal aggression by yelling or name-calling. They also have a hard time finishing tasks that demand patience. Consult a specialist, like a therapist or a doctor, if talking with the child doesn't help.

2.8.4 Bedwetting

Toileting cues may be missed by children who feel insecure or have too much on their minds. When your child has an accident, reassure him that you are not angry. Consult his physician to rule out any medical issues that could be causing his bedwetting.

2.8.5 Hyperactive behavior

When kids are unable to cope with their stress, they throw negative energy. Adults can detect a problem when kids have temper tantrums, running away, or being persistently disobedient. Listening to music, deep breathing exercises, stretching, or yoga can all help your child burn off energy in a calming, positive way.

2.8.6 Backing off from friends and family

A child may feel left out or scared as a result of a divorce, the addition of a new sibling, or harassment at school. To provide comfort, give lots of positive attention and stick to familiar routines. If you assume your child is having problems with her classmates, talk to her teacher.

2.8.7 Sleeping or Eating disorders

When a kid is under stress, anxiety and worry disrupt his or her sleep patterns. Another sign of stress is a dramatic change in their eating habits, whether they start eating more or less. These behaviors can be reduced by reaching the root of his/her anxiety (often with the help of a child counselor or psychologist).

2.8.8 Overreactions to petty problems

The stress to satisfy parents can lead to perfectionist kids with constant worry. Instill confidence in your child so that he can face challenges as well as solve problems on his own.

2.9 Disruptive Mood Dysregulation Disorder (DMDD)

Children are suffering from this disorder act out as they are unable to control their emotions. Irritability and Tantrums are common in childhood, but some children have regular, severe tantrums — even when most children have expanded them — and are irritable all of the time. These are symptoms of a condition known as disruptive mood dysregulation disorder or DMDD. Disruptive means outbursts and tantrums and dysregulation means these kids can't control their sentiments in an age-proper way. Children with DMDD have typically had a tough temperament since infancy. They've struggled with self-calming and adjusting to changes without becoming upset or losing their cool. They were obstinate and hard to control as toddlers. And by the time they reach grade school, they're still throwing tantrums that aren't developmentally appropriate.

Kids with DMDD are generally irritable in between tantrums. They have a short temperament and a low tolerance for frustration. Parents frequently describe living with these children as walking on shells.

2.9.1 What is the causes of these tantrums?

Children with DMDD start out with a lot of strong emotions that they can't control. They are more sensitive to emotions than other children and lack self-control. Tantrums and Irritability are also exacerbated by children with DMDD's. It is because they find it hard to read face expressions. They react by acting out when they notice neutral faces negatively and somewhat

negative faces as severely judgmental or still hostile. Children on the autism spectrum, on the other hand, often do not react to face expressions. They are misunderstood by these kids. When the teacher has pain or is engrossed when she welcomes the kid in the morning, the kid with DMDD becomes alarmed, believing that something is wrong with him. She is angry with me. She's going to chastise me.

2.9.2 What is the difference between DMDD and ODD?

Because the behavior of children with DMDD can resemble that of children with the oppositional defiant disorder, or ODD, the two disorders are frequently confused. They may very well be distracting the classroom by yelling excessively and failing to follow directions. The distinction is that their actions are not intended to defy authority. Clearly, they can't control their emotions, and this is the main problem. Parents, teachers, and psychiatrists will usually describe a child with DMDD as "different," "not actually spiteful," and "not actually vindictive." He can't help himself. And children with DMDD frequently say sorry for their outbursts. They're often taken aback after the tantrums, asking themselves, 'Why did I do this?' A case of DMDD occurs when a child's behavior poses a danger to others. In the heat of the moment, kids with DMDD may throw something without looking where it's going, causing injury to someone. It wasn't, however, his intent. The tantrums of children with DMDD differ from those of typically developing kids on the autism spectrum. An autistic child's tantrum is extra internal. They're attempting to self-soothe in response to a disruption in their own inside environment. It's less vocal, or they keep saying a similar thing. A tantrum in a child with DMDD is more external, targeted at the situation or person that has triggered it.

Typically, it entails shouting at someone or something in protest of something that has been done to them or is being done to them.

2.9.3 How is DMDD diagnosed?

For a DMDD diagnosis, a child must have:

- Extreme anger outbursts, either vocal (shouting), behavioral (physical violence) or both.

- Bursts are out of proportion to the provocation and unsuitable for the child's age.

- The attitude between temper outbursts is angry or irritability for the majority of the day.

- These signs have been present for at least 12 months in almost 3 settings.

- The child cannot be under the age of six or over the age of eighteen, and the start of symptoms must have occurred before the age of ten.

Tantrums are a part of normal development at that age, which is why DMDD can't be diagnosed until a child is six years old; however, parents frequently report that the behavior was there in toddlers. Clinicians don't want to include children who are simply maturing at a slower rate than their peers. And the symptoms must have appeared before the age of ten because if a child exhibits this pattern of symptoms in the 5 grade, it's likely due to something other than DMDD, such as a reaction to adversity at school, at home, or among peers. Children with this pattern of severe irritability and tantrums were diagnosed before with pediatric bipolar disorder until 2014. They were supposed to develop mature bipolar disorder as they grew older, even though their symptoms weren't episodic — mania followed by depression — just like adult bipolar disorder. However, this was not always the case. In fact, like adults, children with DMDD are more likely to have depression or anxiety. Because the emotional extremes can read as fight-or-flight or impulsivity responses, children with DMDD are frequently diagnosed with ADHD or anxiety.

2.9.4 How does DMDD change over time?

As children develop and grow, their DMDD symptoms change. There are many tantrums at school and at home when they are in elementary school. It's possible that the tantrums will continue in central school. When children reach adolescence, tantrums are less about physical outbursts and more about interpersonal conflicts and relationship instability. The lashing out has decreased by early adulthood or late adolescence, but the extreme emotions remain, and they become adopted as depression or anxiety.

2.9.5 How is DMDD treated?

The goal of DMDD treatment is to teach children how to control their emotions and regulate their moods without displaying prolonged or extreme outbursts. These children are frequently treated with parent management training and cognitive behavior therapy, both of which have some success. However, clinicians are now having more success with dialectical behavior therapy or DBT. DBT was initially developed for adults, but it has since been developed for adolescents as well as pre-adolescents. DBT-C or Dialectical Behavioral Therapy for Children, and a modified version known as Mood Masters®, which was developed at the Child Mind Institute, is among the programs for children. In DBT, therapists confirm people's emotions (rather than saying they shouldn't feel that way) and then work with them to develop coping skills for when their emotions become severe to manage. Mindfulness, emotional regulation, distress acceptance, and interpersonal effectiveness skills are taught in both DBT-C and Mood Masters and are linked with parent management training, which educates parents on how to help their children rein in their disturbing behavior. DBT-C, as well as Mood Masters, teach DBT aids to parents as well as kids so that they can practice them with their children — and use them themselves. For school, students can be taught abilities to defuse tense situations, and their IEPs or 504s can be adjusted to adjust them — for example, allowing them to skip the classroom to spray water on their face before returning feeling more in control.

2.10 Medicines Can Be Prescribed Upon Failure Of Therapy And Absence Of Parent Training

Doctors choose to use an antidepressant with fewer side effects, such as an SSRI, to manage the volatile emotions of kids with DMDD. Doctors may give stimulant medicine to help children with top-down self-control. Stimulants help children control their impulses. If that combination of medicines doesn't work, he might try a low-dose atypical antipsychotic like Risperdal. It's not uncommon for clinicians to prescribe Risperdal for children with DMDD when behavioral issues are causing a disaster in the family or at school. This needs to be fixed right away because parents enter with a reason of urgency. They'll be kicked out of school if they don't change their ways, or they'll have to go to residential treatment." Risperdal has serious side effects, so these decisions have to be done carefully. Families dealing with children with DMDD may find it difficult to cope, and this can lead to a lot of disputes between parents. When they're dealing with massive tantrums, changes in child-rearing practices become more apparent, and it can feel like the family is disintegrating. It can be a huge relief to receive a definitive diagnosis. Even mental health specialists struggle to understand children with DMDD. Parents are at a loss for what to do. They can see the light at the end of the tunnel once they understand what it is and what they can do about it — that they are not powerless. It can also be a source of relief for the children. These kids have a lot of potential for growth. It can be exhausting, but once they understand how to manage their condition and regain control, they can be extremely successful and motivated.

Chapter 3: Effective Ways To Help Angry Kids

Unpredictability, a lot of ups and downs, and overall family chaos are all part of raising a child who encounters strong emotions and doesn't yet have the coping mechanisms for dealing with them appropriately. It's not uncommon for parents to feel helpless in the face of their children's constant negative behaviors. Finding your triggers can assist you in assisting an angry child. And Disruptive behaviors and overwhelming noises activate our own unconscious emotions (whether we are informed of them or not) and can quickly destabilize the parenting vision we have. So, how do we stay afloat in the midst of our complex, highly emotional child's chaos while also being the strong parent they require? You must concentrate on yourself. During the child's outbursts and meltdowns, parents must reflect on their own internal states. Putting the focus outward (on the child), and not just on the child but specifically on their behaviors, is very much a part of our parenting culture. While observing a child's behavior can help you better understand the need behind the behavior, the fastest way to achieve peace in your home and the most effective way to help the child deal with anger is to first get your own emotional house in order whether you have a child with an intense temperament or not, you, as the parent set the tone for your family's environment. Your sensitive kid is acutely aware of your energy and is observing and modeling your every move. But don't worry; while the process of self-reflection and emotional management does not happen overnight, there are some simple questions to get you started. The methods to help an angry kid and approaches to anger management for children are listed below.

As the kid with behavioral issues starts to struggle start reflecting on your own behavior

Your sensitive child will experience many emotional ups and downs as a result of his or her intense personality. They'll need you to be their emotional rock while they're young as well as their emotional regulation center is still being built. A calm, confident, and steadfast demeanor that shows you're in it for the long haul (or long meltdown). When it comes to assisting a child with anger, the key is to model your own emotional regulation skills.

You must not be hampered by anything when your child with behavioral problems approaches you in stressful times

Your own subconscious emotions are constantly triggered as a parent of an intense child. These are most likely linked to childhood experiences or internalized mindsets/beliefs over time. Here are a few examples:

"I must stop doing this, I'm condoning this behavior."

"My child must exercise self-control!"

"If my child throws a tantrum, people will think I'm a bad parent."

"She'll never have any mates if she acts like this!"

When you can distinguish your own story from that of your child, you'll be better able to address the needs that underpin their disruptive behaviors while remaining emotionally neutral as well as supportive.

You need to assist your child in moments of anger and extend him your full support

When your brain's stress center is under attack, planning ahead of time how to increase your chances of success during difficult parenting situations will go a long way to helping you. Here are some recommendations:

- Make a mantra that you can recite whenever you're feeling stressed

- Make visuals with your parenting intentions to hang around your house

- Make a daily parenting intention to keep it fresh in your mind

You will not always be able to control rapidly rising stress hormones and an over-activated amygdala due to the pesky fact that you are human. Negative thoughts will not help you be a strong and stable parent for your intense child, so plan to practice self-compassion and take time to repair as well as connect with your child

3.1 Types of Anger Issues

Anger can be manifested in several different ways with different intensity levels:

3.1.1 Inward Anger

Internally directed anger could include bleak and miserable thoughts as well as negative self-discussion. Punishing yourself is typically associated with inward anger, such as depriving yourself of activities you enjoy, like watching television or exercising. It may even imply depriving yourself of basic necessities such as food and water.

3.1.2 Outward Anger

This entails verbally or physically expressing your anger and frustration toward other people or things. It can include damaging property and assaulting others, as well as screaming and cursing.

3.1.3 Passive Anger

Acts like being sarcastic or insulting toward others, giving others silent treatment, and sulking are examples of passive-aggressive behavior.

3.2 Helping a kid to Deal with his Anger

Anger is a basic emotion that all individuals experience, but it's a little more complicated because it frequently manifests as a secondary emotion as a result of an emotional reaction to the other emotion. This is also why the phrase "anger is a mask" comes to mind: under the anger, there are often other complex emotions. For a variety of reasons, your child's anger is fast to come to the save:

- Anger is an adaptive emotion for humans, indicating a

potential threat, assisting communication, and pushing us toward goal-focused behavior.

- Anger is quick to describe than more deep as well as weak emotions, giving us the false notion of energy and control in a situation where we're most likely feeling vulnerable and weak.

- Because their frontal lobe and cortex are still developing, kids are much more spontaneous with their emotions.

Anger is a natural human reaction that can be useful and effective in certain situations, such as responding to threats of harm to yourself and others. Anger management issues, on the other hand, can be destructive as well as cause problems in your life, as well as have a negative impact on personal and professional relationships. Anger has a negative impact not only on your external relationships but also on your health. According to studies, being unable to manage your anger can take to heart disease, bulimia, diabetes, and car accidents. When assisting people with anger management issues, it is critical to consider both psychological and medicinal treatments. Anger is caused by a variety of internal and external factors. Mental instability and depression are examples of internal factors. External factors, on the other hand, might include situations that cause stress or anxiety, as well as financial or professional issues, as well as family and relationship issues. Consider assisting your child in dealing with rage as a journey rather than a destination. To nurture strong relationships with their emotions, particularly complex ones like rage, children will require ongoing support and instruction. These anger management methods will give you peace of mind that you're giving your kid a strong roadmap for dealing with anger, both now and in the future. The most important factor in

determining how your child will thrive in the world with themselves and others is to support their emotional well-being.

When anger is not correctly understood and dealt with, it can lead to increased stress, relationship conflict, behavioral troubles, and aggression, among other things. Anger is a healthy and normal human emotion for a child to experience, and the sooner they develop a positive relationship with it, the better equipped they will be to adapt to life's challenges, staying in control of anger rather than allowing anger to control them.

3.2.1 Be proactive

In the midst of a disaster or an argument, talking about intense emotions is a waste of time. This is because your child will not get or recall much (if anything) of what you say if they are in a state of high emotional arousal. We know that when the emotional core of the brain is overactive, the connection with the brain's thinking part is lost. This is why the mind goes totally blank before a presentation, though it happens on a much larger scale when you're angry. Allow your child to speak about emotions as well as coping abilities for anger on a regular basis in everyday life so that he or she can adopt these transforming skills to memory. Before the child gets angry, it is necessary to work together to make a strategy for how to cool down.

3.2.2 Give your kid a lifeline

The most effective way to assist an angry kid is for you, the parent, to remain calm. A child's greatest fear, aside from experiencing strong emotions, is witnessing a parent lose control. You are your child's guide, and they rely on you to keep them in check when they can't. You shouldn't expect your child to hold you accountable if you can't hold yourself responsible when your emotions are getting high.

3.2.3 Explore your kid's triggers

Helping your child think about what usually happens before "their anger arises" is a great way to help them develop self-knowledge and be better ready for when difficult situations arise again.

3.2.4 Teach the kid emotion vocabulary

When you give your child a broad range of emotion vocabulary, you give them a way to help you better understand what they're going through and how can they express it appropriately. It might be be difficult for your kid to recognize and understand an emotion if they are unaware that it even exists.

3.2.5 Team up

While you might expect your child to calm down on their own, most children will require the good support of his parent or caretaker to work through the anger and cool and control their nervous system. Co-regulation is an important part of parenting an emotionally intelligent kid who can handle their anger well in adulthood. It involves supporting the child through the wave of anger and experimenting with what helps them recover emotional stability through trial and error.

3.2.6 Explain through modeling

When you're angry, your kid is watching you see how you react to anger. Do you spend most of your time modeling self-control and coping policies, or do you let your emotions control your actions and words? Modeling and practicing healthy coping skills in front of your child is the most effective way to teach them how to deal with anger in a positive way. So, the next time your kid breaks a glass of milk, press pause and take 5 deep breaths.

3.2.7 Body threatening signs

Helping a child build self-awareness about their bodies' natural reactions to anger is an important part of supporting their emotional regulation skills. If your kid can recognize the physical signs of anger in their bodies, they can use calming strategies before the anger takes over. Assist them in examining how they experience anger in their bodies during an angry explosion. Does their face become flushed and hot as a result of this? Do their muscles tense up, or do they hold their breath? These are important hints to help your kid deal with his or her anger.

3.2.8 Use visuals

Visuals will be your best friend when your kid is in the midst of an angry outburst. When your child is upset, it's much easier for them to visually process info than it is for them to process what you say because of what's going on in their brain during the emotional upheaval. Because their thoughtful brain is closed, the more essential the intervention, the more likely it will be tolerated and effective by your child.

3.2.9 Help the kid become conscious of their anger

It's easy for parents to jump in and tell their children to "get over it" when they're experiencing strong emotions. This is particularly true when it comes to the emotion of anger. Even the most loving parents are attracted to instruct and advise their children. Our children, on the other hand, have a difficult time listening to anyone when they are experiencing strong emotions. Our children don't want criticism or advice; they just want to be grasped. They want us to fully comprehend their emotions. Many parents have discovered that simply sitting down and listening to their children is enough to help them release their anger. Be sure you talk to your kids at the appropriate time. When considering the personality categories, most extroverts prefer to process information externally. They prefer to discuss issues right away. The majority of introverts would want to process information internally. They prefer to consider it before speaking about it. Being insensitive to the child's preferred method of expressing anger will only add to his or her frustration, making it more difficult, if not impossible, to deal with. You'll eventually be able to help the children find other ways to express their anger. When your kids say, "I'm angry," you can ask, "Do you ponder your anger comes from being scared, frustrated, or hurt?"

3.2.10 Model suitable anger management skills

The best way to teach children how to deal with anger is to

demonstrate how you deal with emotions when you're angry. Children are more likely to lose their cool if they see you lose yours. They will, however, notice if you are kinder and gentler with your emotions. While it is critical to protect children from the majority of adult problems, it is also beneficial to demonstrate how you handle anger. Make a point of citing times when you're frustrated so that the child understands that adults can be angry as well. It's acceptable to say, "I'm angry that the car in front of us didn't stop to let those kids cross the street." But I'm going to come to a complete stop so they can cross safely." If you express your feelings verbally, your children would then learn to talk about them. Also, accept responsibility for your actions if you lose your cool in front of your children. Instead, make an apology as well as talk about what you've done. "I'm sorry you had to witness me yelling when I was angry today," they say. I should have gone for a walk to let off steam instead of raising my voice."

3.2.11 Establish anger rules

When it comes to anger, most families have unspoken rules about what

behavior is acceptable and what is not. Some families don't mind slamming doors and raising voices, while others have a lower tolerance for such behavior. Create a set of written house rules that spell out your expectations. The focus of anger rules should be on treating others with respect. Deal with issues like physical aggression, name-calling, and property destruction so that your students know they cannot throw or break things or react physically or verbally when they are upset.

3.2.12 Teach healthy coping skills

Children must learn how to manage their anger in appropriate ways. Rather than being told, "Don't hit your brother," show them what they could do when they're frustrated. "Next time, use the words" or "When you're angry, walk away from him." "What could you do rather than hitting?" is another question you can ask to help your kid think of alternative strategies. You could also make a calming kit that they can use when they're upset. Fill a box with items that will help them relax, like a coloring book and crayons, scented lotion, or relaxing music. You have to engage their senses to relax their mind and body. Use time-outs to assist your child in calming down. Teach them that if they get into trouble, they could still take a time-out. For children who are prone to anger, removing them from a situation as well as taking a few minutes to calm down could be extremely beneficial.

3.2.13 Teach healthy coping skills

Children should learn how to handle their anger in suitable ways. Instead of telling them "Don't hit your brother," tell them better ways which they can adopt while angry. "When you're angry, walk away from him" or "Next time, use the words." "What could you do rather than hitting?" are some of the things you can ask in order to help your kid acknowledge the alternative strategies. You can also make a calming kit for your kid that they might use when they're angry or upset about something. Take a box and put items in it that will help your kid relax, for example scented lotion, crayons and a coloring book, or relaxing music. You have to help them by engaging their senses for relaxing their body and mind. Use time-outs to help them in calming down. Tell your kid that if he gets into trouble

sometime, he could still take a time-out. For kids who are prone to anger, taking some time to calm down or taking them out from the situation could be extremely helpful.

3.3 How To Discipline A Child With Anger Issues?

You're probably left wondering how to discipline your child as you figure out the actual reasons for their rage. When you're dealing with anger issues, discipline takes different forms. When your child is struggling to control their anger, you don't need to get angry at them. What they require is validation and guidance on how to channel that energy in a constructive manner.

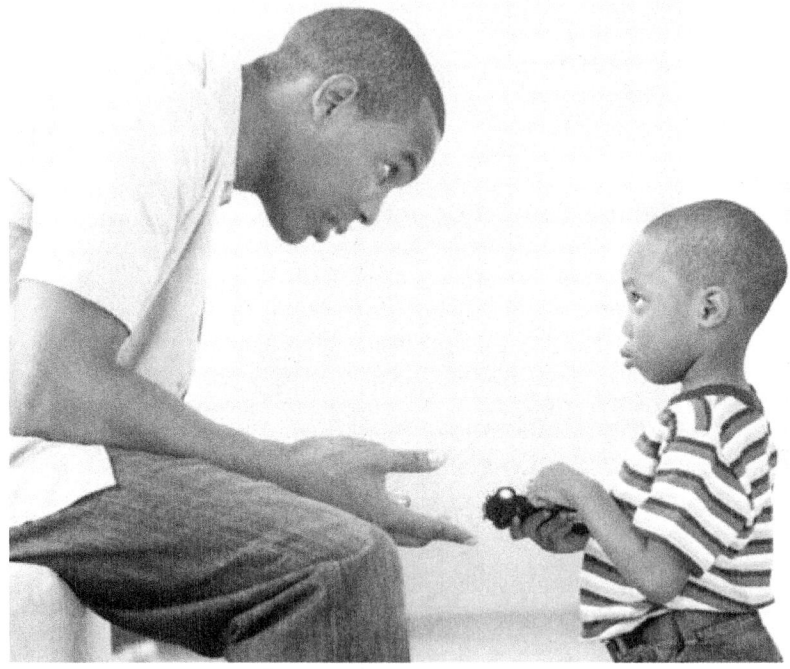

Tips for disciplining your angry child

- Make an effort to maintain a calm demeanor when approaching your kids. They sense your energy directed at them, and if you are angry, the situation will only get worse.

- Help them relax by reminding them that it's fine to be angry, but it's not okay to be mean or belligerent in their anger. Make them understand that while they will be able to "feel" the emotion, you will assist them in finding other ways to relax.

- Give them some techniques for self-soothing. You can give them a drawing book to help them get over their anger.

Bottom line

Although this may take some time to figure out the real reasons for your child's anger, don't give up. Your child requires your attention now more than ever, and there is hope at the end of the tunnel. You are showing your children that they are not alone by setting an example for them, loving them, and trying for the solution to their problems.

Conclusion

While anger is a natural and healthy emotion, many children experience it to a greater and greater extent, resulting in significant stress for the child and the family. The first step toward guiding your angry child toward a new, better relationship with anger is to investigate the underlying issues that may be affecting them beneath the surface. Your child's anger loves deceiving you. It might make you feel out of control, helpless, and hopeless (and like you're failing as a parent), but the reality about anger must be remembered. We may gain a deeper understanding of it and the role it provides for your child (to help them survive and cope with difficult situations) without enabling it to take control. Accepting and treating anger in a healthy and confident manner where we are in charge of it, rather than the other way around, might set the stage for your child to have a healthy relationship with anger. If your child is having frequent anger issues that are creating substantial stress at school, with peers, or at home, you should get him or her assessed by a mental health specialist. You should take prompt action and treat your child's anger issues as soon as possible.

Printed in Great Britain
by Amazon

80717105R00037